TABLE OF CONTENTS

Introduction

In December 2005, the film *Laylat Soqoot Baghdad (The Night Baghdad Fell)* was released in Egypt proposing a future of American imperialism in the Middle East. Replete with scenes of destroyed national landmarks, a desolate Cairo city, and an Abu Ghraib-like prison facility, the film depicts the fall of Egypt to American Invaders. The film's director, Mohamed Amin, says *Laylat Soqoot Baghdad* is an anti-American movie arguing the United States is "the main catalyst" of conflict in most parts of the world. Discussing the film, a prominent Arab political analyst maintained American foreign policy is arrogant and "devised to humiliate Arabs and Muslims."[1] That anti-American sentiment has grown in the Arab world is not surprising given the United States' support to Israel and recent military operations in the Middle East. Twenty years ago this story probably would have never been heard in the West, today, however, this story and countless others like it are propagated to hundreds of millions of people across the world.

The evolution of communications has given global voice to unprecedented numbers of people with myriad diverse agendas. The World Trade Organization (WTO) witnessed this emergence first-hand in 1999. Organized through the internet, anti-globalization groups merged with numerous disparate environmental and human rights groups to protest the WTO's annual meeting in Seattle. The number of protesters and the publicity they generated were sufficient to undermine consensus and prevented completion of a WTO agreement.[2] Individuals previously marginalized or limited by conventional media communications now aggregate into like-minded virtual communities capable of international influence.[3]

---

[1] Amira Howeidy, "After Baghdad, Is Cairo Next?" *Al Jazeera*, 18 January 2006, http://english.aljazeera.net/English/Archive/Archive?ArchiveID=17755, (accessed 19 September 2007).

[2] Douglas Kellner, "Theorizing Globalization," *Sociology Theory* 20, no. 3 (November 2002): 296.

[3] Tom Price, *Cyber Activism: Advocacy Groups and the Internet* (Washington, D.C.: Foundation for Public Affairs, 2000), 31.

In parallel with this evolution, America has risen to prominence as the world's most dominant and influential nation. These two nearly simultaneous events created large numbers of people suspicious of American hegemony and armed with the means to be heard on a global scale. Many of these individuals go so far as to characterize the United States as a rogue nation, "the greatest colossus in history, no longer bound by international law, the concerns of allies, or any constraints on its use of military force."[4] Proponents of this rogue-America theory cite as evidence of rogue intent America's support to nations with deficient human rights records (e.g. Indonesia) or conflict with neighboring states (e.g. Colombia). The reemergence of the primacy of the military in American foreign policy implementation further fuels this argument in harkening historical evidence of militaries as tools of tyranny and oppression. Above all, rogue-America proponents cite America's stated readiness to use its tremendous power in defense of its sovereignty, unilaterally if necessary, as evidence that it is the most dangerous of rogue states.[5] Yet for all the rogue-America rhetoric, nothing in American policies, speeches or other public positions suggest the motives of a rogue nation. In the absence of explicit evidence of rogue intent, why do accusations of an American rogue state persist? Should the United States even be concerned with rogue-America rhetoric?[6]

What if such rogue-like characterizations were ascribed to the United States by overwhelming numbers of governments or coalitions that include major western powers? Is it possible for America to be cast into isolation with the likes of North Korea? Even if the United States were not shunned by the current world order, is it possible for other world powers to exploit rogue-America rhetoric to build a competing world order?

---

[4] Chalmers Johnson, *The Sorrows of Empire* (New York: Metropolitan Books), 3.

[5] Noam Chomsky, *Rogue States* (Cambridge: South End Press, 2000), 4.

[6] For more on rogue-America rhetoric see also William Blum's *Rogue State: A Guide to the World's Only Superpower,* Carl Boggs' *Masters of War;* Chalmers Johnson's *Blowback;* Michael Mann's *Incoherent Empire*; and Stephen Kinzer's *Overthrow.*

While hard to imagine either future, trends for each possibility are clearly underway today. Trends to the latter future are evident in Russia and China where each promotes a new world order supported by language arguing the United States is a dangerous global hegemon.[7] A trend toward the former future is evident in the European Union and other traditional friends and allies. In January 2003, as war with Iraq seemed inevitable, the External Relations Commissioner of the European Union stated in a speech at Oxford, England "to assert the primacy of U.S. concerns...constitutes a threat not just to the developing international order, but to the U.S. itself."[8] The perception of the United States as a threat to the very international order it was so instrumental in creating is troubling. That this perception was voiced by the lead foreign policy professional of an international body prominent in the global architecture should be cause for concern to American policy-makers.

The United States should be concerned with trends toward American marginalization, or trends of competing powers to exploit rogue-America rhetoric as either could produce economic and security shocks on a global scale. United States foreign policy should be shaped with an understanding of how American actions could be perceived as those of a rogue nation by the world community. Such an informed foreign policy will allow the United States to avert rogue actions or mitigate rogue perceptions through clearly articulated communications.

The latter half of the twentieth century saw expansion of the United States military in American foreign policy. American military operations in Korea, Vietnam, Grenada, Panama, Somalia, Haiti, the Balkans, Sudan, Afghanistan and Iraq are often cited as evidence the Untied States' foreign policy has become overly militaristic in resolving crises.[9] Some proponents of rogue-America theory couple these events with America's legacy of support to less-than-

---

[7] A discussion of the security strategies of China and Russia is included in section II, pages 30-31 of this paper.

[8] Chris Patten, (Cyril Foster Lecture, Balliol College, Oxford, 30 January 2003), http://ec.europa.eu/external_relations/news/patten/oxford300103.htm (accessed 14 December 2007).

[9] William Blum, *Killing Hope* (Monroe: Common Courage Press, 1995), 9-20.

3

democratic regimes (e.g. Colombia, Indonesia, Pakistan, Israel, Saudi Arabia) as evidence of America's dedication to the rule of force, its indifference to world opinion, and arrogant unilateralism.[10] Many critics go so far as to argue the United States has itself become a rogue state worthy of global isolation. But is there a legitimate basis for the characterization of America as a rogue state, and should the United States even care if it is so characterized?

This paper proposes that while there is a trend toward an overly militaristic American foreign policy, this trend is due more to the American military's responsiveness and capacity to accomplish non-military activities than a rogue state strategy dedicated to the rule of force. American strategic communications, however, have been ineffectual in articulating this distinction: overcoming the stigma associated with militaries as instruments of oppression and conveying to the world a concise, sustained and positive message of its National strategy. Misunderstanding American intent, other nations are increasingly viewing the United States as a "rogue superpower."[11] To mitigate and reverse this perception, the American government must first understand how its actions have, or could have contributed to it. Armed with such an understanding, American leaders can then make informed decisions on foreign policy actions (or lack of action) and mitigate or avert perceptions of rogue intent through concise communications to the contrary.

Framework

This analysis begins with an exploration of what ramifications might arise from worldwide perception of a rogue America. From this basis the paper then defines what characteristics constitute a rogue state and explore the correlation between imperialism, military, and the use of the military that could result in the perception of rogue state. The paper then

---

[10] Chomsky, *Rogue States*, 2-5; Stephen Kinzer, *Overthrow* (New York: Henry Holt and Company, 2006), 239.

[11] Samuel P. Huntington, "The Lonely Superpower," *Foreign Policy* 78, no. 2 (March/April 1999): 42.

proceeds to explore historical behaviors in American foreign policy that exhibit rogue-like traits and highlights two prevalent trends in exploiting these traits with rhetoric to advance regional agendas or alternatives to the existing international order. The paper concludes with a discussion of actions the American government can undertake to avert or minimize the rogue state label.

This paper will not address the appropriateness of using the military to accomplish non-military foreign policy objectives as such decisions are informed by each unique situation and are solely the prerogative of the National Command Authorities of the United States. Rather, this paper accepts military employment to accomplish non-military aspects of National power as a reality of the current state of America and the international security environment. However, the paper does explore the ramifications of this militaristic approach to foreign policy as a means of emphasizing the prudence of rigorous debate and vigilant communications when contemplating military employment and the positive role these actions can make in mitigating or averting the rogue-America rhetoric.

Ramifications of a Rogue America

The idea of the United States as a beacon of democracy, a shining light of liberty before the world has endured throughout America's history.[12] Fundamental to this perception are the values America touts as fundamental to its character: the rule of law, individual liberty and respect for human rights.[13] Yet it is with these same values rogue-America pundits attack American foreign policy actions. If the United States were successfully isolated as a rogue nation, or marginalized by rogue rhetoric, it would lose its ability to influence global security and economics.

---

[12] Michael Dunne, "Hemisphere and the Globe: the Terms of American Foreign Relations," *International Affairs* 70, no. 4 (October 1994): 704.

[13] President. *The National Security Strategy of the United States of America* (March 2006): 2.

America risks becoming marginalized or even isolated if it were considered a rogue state in the world community. If the United States were subsequently removed from influence in world affairs in the way of Cuba, Burma, or North Korea, an era of instability and conflict would ensue. The global effects of such an eventuality are elaborated below, but in short, isolating the United States from the very world order it was so instrumental in creating, and is so instrumental in sustaining, would produce economic and security shocks on a global scale.

The Global Economy Without the U.S.

In 1997, speculation on the Thai baht drove its value down thirty percent and set off a global market meltdown that rippled throughout Asia to Russia, then South America. Only as the repercussions continued into the United States did world economists begin to comprehend the complex international dynamic that was the global economy. Paradoxically, the more economists learn about this new dynamic, the more they "don't fully understand how it works."[14] Most recently, a crisis in American home mortgages led to radical drops in Asian and European markets and led some financial experts to conclude a global recession was imminent.[15]

Globalization has made international relations more important than at any other period in world history. So intertwined and complex are the economic interests of world nations that cause and effect, event and impact, are virtually indistinguishable at the national level but nonetheless recognizable throughout the world community. Thus, American interests permeate all aspects of the global economy.[16] To this world economy, the United States and the European Union contribute equal shares comprising forty percent of the world's total trade. Additionally, they

---

[14] Thomas L. Friedman, *The Lexus and the Olive Tree* (New York: Farrar, Straus, Giroux, 1999), 368.

[15] Landon Thomas, "Dread of American Downturn Goes Global," *Kansas City Star,* 22 January 2008, A1.

[16] For more on the complexities of globalization and the role of the United States in the globalized world order see Thomas Freidman's *The World is Flat,* or George Soros' *The Bubble of American Supremacy.*

combine to generate fifty-seven percent of world economic output.[17] With just half the population of the European Union however, the United States is clearly the power broker in the global economy.

Hence, isolation of the United States from the world community would devastate the American economy as trading partners around the world would be compelled to divest themselves of American interests. More importantly, removal of one fifth of the world's trade and over a quarter of its economic output would not only induce an international economic downturn, but also imperil global security. The potential for American foreign policy to induce such a shock may not be as remote as some would wish. In address at Oxford in January 2003, the Foreign Minister to the European Union cautioned:

> "the instinct to return to a narrow definition of the national interest – to assert the primacy of US concerns, and especially economic interests, over any outside authority – constitutes a threat not just to the developing international order, but to the US itself."[18]

In short, the United States is "nothing without the rest of the world, and the world cannot thrive without [it]."[19]

But globalization and America's prominence in it are not self-perpetuating. Indeed, lest one conclude economic interdependence will preclude American isolation by the world community, history proves otherwise. Realist political scientist John Mearsheimer notes that economic interdependence in Europe was as great in 1914 as it is today, yet did nothing to deter the Great Powers from plunging into World War I.[20] To be sure, ensuring the security of the

---

[17] Benita Ferrero-Waldner, "Opportunities and Challenges in the EU-US Relationship," (lecture, French-American Foundation, New York, 28 September 2007), http://www.eurunion.org/news/press/2005/2005006.htm (accessed 14 December 2007).

[18] Patten, Oxford, 30 January 2003.

[19] Friedman, *Lexus and the Olive Tree*, 372.

[20] John Mearsheimer, *The Tragedy of Great Power Politics* (New York: W.W. Norton & Company, 2001), 371.

global economic order is no longer a given, nor is it merely an imperative of American National interest. Rather, protecting the global economy is an issue of global security as well.

Global Security

The second half of the twentieth century was characterized as a bipolar power struggle between the United States and the Soviet Union. While this period saw several proxy conflicts between the two powers, major regional conflict was largely averted due to the inherent stability of a bipolar security arrangement brokered by nuclear deterrence. In this system, each power dominated a coalition in security competition with the other. Limited conflicts occurred where these two powers struggled for influence over non-aligned countries. But the demise of the Soviet Union upset this balanced global security environment[21] and, since the United States lacks the power and National will to assume the mantle of global hegemon, resulted in the uni-multipolar system in existence today: a world political scientist Samuel Huntington describes as one with a single superpower and major powers in regions throughout the world.[22]

In this dynamic, the United States maintains dominance in all instruments of national power, and it maintains the capacity to project that power globally. Major regional powers (German-French condominium, China, India, Iran, Brazil, and South Africa) enjoy increased influence in their respective areas of the globe but have only limited ability to project power. Unique amongst major regional powers, Russia's regional influence has decreased as a result of the Soviet Union's fall, but still maintains sufficient power to dominate its region of the world.[23]

Beneath this layer of major powers are competitors for influence in the region. Britain, Ukraine, Japan, South Korea, Pakistan, Saudi Arabia, Argentina and Venezuela all maintain, or continue to improve their power relative to their respective regions, and their interests are

---

[21] Mearsheimer, *Tragedy of Great Power Politics*, 335, 361.

[22] Huntington, "The Lonely Superpower," 36.

[23] Ibid.

frequently at odds with the other major powers in those regions.[24] Suppression of, or aggression by, these potential competitors for regional supremacy is typically kept in check by the power of the United States. As liberalist political scientist Joseph Nye observes, "the American role as a stabilizer and reassurance against aggression by aspiring hegemons in key regions is a blue chip issue."[25]

But this uni-multipolar system is being challenged by a world increasingly suspicious of America's power. Were the United States to be isolated from the international order as a "rogue superpower," an unbalanced multipolar situation would emerge creating the most unstable of possible power structures not unlike the situation prior to World War II. Such an unbalanced multipolar world could see an increase in conflict as major powers vied with peer competitors for regional supremacy.[26] It is not beyond reason to envision one or more of the following scenarios coming to pass in this new world order:

This dynamic could see Japan rising to challenge China's bid for regional hegemony, and putting neither in a position to challenge North Korean aggression against its southern neighbor. Britain's reluctance to intervene might sway Russia's decision to reassert itself in Eastern Europe, challenged only if Germany and France could summon the national will to resist.[27] Without the benefit of American aid to Israel, Egypt and Saudi Arabia, Iran could consolidate its power in the Middle East and the world's largest source of oil. Saudi Arabian leadership would be undermined to the point it could become a failing state and Israel would likely cease to exist.[28] In the Western Hemisphere, the situation might be slightly better, though tensions between Brazil

---

[24] Huntington, "The Lonely Superpower," 36.

[25] Joseph S. Nye, *The Paradox of American Power* (New York: Oxford University Press, 2002), 144.

[26] Mearsheimer, *Tragedy of Great Power Politics*, 355, 361-362.

[27] Ibid, 392-400.

[28] Simon Henderson, "Saudi Arabia: the Nightmare of Iraq," *With Neighbors Like These,* Policy Focus #70 (The Washington Institute for Near East Policy, June 2007): 41.

and Argentina would surely arise in keeping with their long history of conflict. Venezuela might also seize the opportunity to foment dissent in, or threaten Colombia and Ecuador.

Just as the nations of the world are economically interdependent, so too is their individual security dependent on the security of other nations. Key to both continued economic growth and global security is the continued participation and leadership of the United States in the world order. As American Thomas Friedman observes, "in this world we can't afford either isolation or waiting around for some smaller adversary to become a life-threatening foe."[29]

American Behavior and the Rhetoric of Rogue

> "I dread our own power, and our own ambition; I dread our being too much dreaded ….to hold the commerce of all other nations totally dependent upon our good pleasure, we may say that we shall not abuse this astonishing and hitherto unheard-of-power. But every other nation will think we shall abuse it. It is impossible but that, sooner or later, this state of things must produce a combination against us which may end in our ruin."
>
> -- Edmund Burke[30]

The end of the Cold War marked the end of America's evolution as the world's only superpower that began at the dawn of the twentieth century. The American foreign policy evolutions facilitating this rise were founded on the fundamental belief the United States "has a responsibility to nurture democracy and economic growth around the world" and "that the interests of democracies… could never conflict with those of humanity."[31] As America's influence spread across the globe, so too did its military presence, preserving regional stability and promoting the interests of the United States and its nascent democratic allies. The end of the Cold War, however, saw the creation of the global order previously discussed, and America's

---

[29] Friedman, *Lexus and the Olive Tree*, 372.

[30] Edmund Burke, "Remarks on the Policy of the Allies With Respect to France," *The Works of the Right Honourable Edmund Burke Vol. III* (London: George Bell and Sons, 1887), 448.

[31] Walter A. McDougall, *Promised Land, Crusader State* (Boston: Houghton Mifflin Company, 1997), 5, 124.

1991 success in repelling Iraq's invasion of Kuwait reaffirmed American military prowess. These two events and an American outlook girded with the belief that America must "go forth and do good among nations" set the stage for a decade of incoherent and ever-changing foreign policy as the United States sought to understand its role in this new world order.[32]

Further compounding America's quest for a new and coherent foreign policy was its efforts to contain Saddam Hussein's post Gulf-War Iraq.[33] As diplomacy and soft power brought little or no success in bringing Hussein's regime to heel, a new National security concept emerged. A strategy to contain outlaw nations like those of Iraq and North Korea was combined with counterterrorism strategies from the previous decade to produce the "rogue state" doctrine, the new centerpiece of American National security strategy.[34]

So what exactly constitutes a rogue state? The body of interpretations that characterizes a rogue state is vast, nuanced, and continues to evolve. Hence, it is best to begin by examining a formal definition of rogue. The Merriam Webster American Collegiate dictionary defines a rogue as "vicious and destructive; isolated and dangerous or uncontrollable."[35] Applied to a sovereign nation, then, the term suggests a state prone to violence, removed from the world order, unbounded by the structures of, and a threat to that order.

Many of the world's perceptions of the rogue state began taking shape in the late 1970's and early 1980's. At the time, journalists used terms such as "rogue regime" to describe states that "commit unspeakable crimes against their people," and political analysts described states that

---

[32] McDougall, *Promised Land, Crusader State*, 11; Dale R. Herspring, *The Pentagon and the Presidency* (Lawrence: University Press of Kansas, 2005), 373.

[33] Linda B. Miller, "The Clinton Years: Reinventing US Foreign Policy," *International Affairs* 70, no. 4 (October 1994): 621-622.

[34] Anthony Lake, "The Reach of Democracy: Tying Power to Diplomacy," *The New York Times,* 23 September 1994, http://query.nytimes.com/gst/fullpage.html?res=9D07E3D7143AF930A1575AC0A962958260&sec=&spon=&pagewanted=2 (accessed 21 January 2008).

[35] Merriam Webster's Online Dictionary, http://www.m-w.com/dictionary/rogue.

were marginalized or politically isolated as "pariah states."[36] Hence, while the notion of rogue

states is not new, today the term itself is an artifice of post-Cold War American foreign policy.

Former American National Security Advisor Anthony Lake was first to coin the phrase and

established the containment of rogue states as a key fixture in the foreign policy of the United

States. In 1994, he defined these as states which "seek to traffic in the weapons of mass

destruction, support terrorism and are dedicated to the destruction of the tolerant society."[37] The

2002 National Security Strategy of the United States elaborated that rogue states "brutalize their

own people… display no regard for international law, threaten their neighbors, and callously

violate international treaties to which they are party…are determined to acquire weapons of mass

destruction…sponsor terrorism around the globe and reject basic human values."[38]

Convoluting a precise rogue state definition are rogue-America pundits fashioning the

definition for convenience in making their argument. Focusing his attention on the United States,

linguistics professor Noam Chomsky limits his rogue state definition to a state "that defies

international laws and conventions [and] does not consider itself bound by the major treaties and

conventions."[39] Pascal Boniface, Executive Director of France's *Institute of International and

Strategic Relations,* likened rogue states to the biblical David in defining them as "one that rises

against the United States without really having the means to do so."[40]

Therefore, any attempt to derive a precise definition would only serve to invite legalistic

debate to arrive at a subjective standard with which to judge whether a particular entity is, or is

---

[36] Robert S. Litwak, *Rogue States and U.S. Foreign Policy* (Washington D.C.: Woodrow Wilson Center Press, 2000), 50-52.

[37] Lake, "The Reach of Democracy."

[38] President. *The National Security Strategy of the United States of America* (September 2002): 14.

[39] Noam Chomsky, "Rogue States Draw the Usual Line," *The Noam Chomsky Website,* May 2001, http://www.chomsky.info/interviews/200105--.htm (accessed 3 August 2007).

[40] Pascal Boniface, "Reflections on America As A World Power: A Eurpoean View," *Journal of Palestine Studies* 29, no. 3 (Spring 2000): 10.

not a rogue state.[41] Rather than attempt to arrive at such definitive judgment, for the purposes of this paper it is more beneficial to amalgamate commonly accepted rogue traits from myriad sources in order to determine what behaviors are most likely to be interpreted as rogue-like. American foreign policy behavior will then be compared with this amalgamated rogue character to assess the strengths and weaknesses of the rogue-America thesis.

Following, then, is an analysis of regimes from history which exemplified roguish traits. These include great empires, dictatorships, and modern states to which the rogue label has been affixed. Additionally, other modern states are analyzed to assess why they have not been labeled rogue despite demonstrating some rogue-like qualities. From this sampling, an amalgamation of rogue characteristics will be codified.

The militaristic and self-interested behavior commonly understood to be rogue-like is not unlike that of historical empires. Examining empires from Greece to Rome, Persia to Great Britain, all were characterized by the self-interests of wealth and state security, and each employed their respective militaries to preserve those interests. However, history also shows these empires brought much to the evolution of human civilizations. Advancements in medicine, mathematics, physics, engineering, public sanitation, formal education and interstate commerce are but a few examples of the contributions past empires have made to human civilization.[42] Most important to note is that civilization's great empires brought order and diplomacy to higher levels of importance in foreign relations, so ascribing dedication to the rule of force to historical empires is tenuous at best. Further, the increased role of diplomacy suggests anything but roguish self-interest pursued in isolation.

---

[41] According to political scientist Alexander George, the term "rogue state" has no basis in international law, so its use has led to significant friction between the United States and the international community in developing policy and strategies to deal with so-called rogue states. For a complete examination on the legal implications of the rogue state designation, a paper on the subject can be found at the German Law Journal website http://www.germanlawjournal.com/article.php?id=188.

[42] Public Broadcasting Service, *Empires,* 2008, http://www.pbs.org/empires/ (accessed 30 January 2008).

Hence, isolation and rule of force are the key discriminators between rogue states and empires, and a history of imperialistic action is not a singularly sufficient condition for rogue nation status. Empires of the past, however, benefit from a retrospective analysis of their benevolent contributions over the long-term. Without such benefit, it is difficult to draw distinction between the actions of past empires with those of today's rogue states. Expeditionary or constabulary militaries remain an enduring symbol of the tyranny and oppression associated with self-interested empires.

Beyond empires, history offers other examples of sovereign behavior generally considered roguish, and repressive dictatorships represent an intuitive area in further refining the rogue state definition. The regimes of Cambodia's Pol Pot and Uganda's Idi Amin orchestrated oppressive and brutal campaigns within their countries as means of consolidating their power. From 1975 to 1979, Pol Pot's Khmer Rouge commenced a campaign to purge Cambodia of the trappings of Western influence. Over one million people were killed or executed in the purges, and ethnic Vietnamese were specifically targeted. In December 1978, following attacks on Vietnamese border villages, Vietnamese forces overthrew the Khmer Rouge and ended their reign of terror. Similarly, by 1979, the Ugandan people had endured brutal atrocities that included some 300,000 deaths at the hands of dictator Idi Amin. The slaughter ended only after Tanzania overran the country following an incursion into its border by Ugandan forces.[43]

At the height of the Cold War, abusing one's own people was sufficient to garner roguish descriptors from a horrified world community, and sometimes this behavior was met with censure of the offending country by one of its neighbors. As a whole, however, human rights abuses were insufficient to earn international censure and isolation. In fact, while Pol Pot's atrocities drew little or no action from the world community, Vietnamese violation of Cambodia's sovereign borders drew censure from the United Nations and diplomatic isolation of the new Cambodian

---

[43] Sean D. Murphy, *Humanitarian Intervention: the United Nations in an Evolving World Order* (Philadelphia: University of Pennsylvania Press, 1996), 103-105.

government.[44] Left in the wake of these often brutal armed occupations is a lingering sense of suspicion in many parts of the world that militaries are the instruments of tyranny. Oppressive dictators who used their military to control the populace, threaten their neighbors, or control conquered populations rise to the top of candidates for rogue status. But history indicates states had to display more aberrant behavior to be ostracized from the world order as a rogue nation.[45] Such aberrant behavior characterized the regimes of Stalinist Russia and Nazi Germany.

It has been estimated that between 1929 and 1953, Joseph Stalin's great terror in the Soviet Union was responsible for over twenty million deaths due to forced labor, collectivization, execution, and terrorism, and half of these deaths occurred by the Summer of 1935. Further, the average population of forced labor camps in the gulag was 8.8 million over the same period.[46] However, Stalin's regime did not garner international censure in spite of these atrocities as it was not deemed a threat to its neighbors (at the time) and was a crucial ally in the war against the true rogue regime of the period, that of Adolph Hitler.

Adolph Hitler's regime was among the worst examples of oppression in the twentieth century where he carried out a horrifying campaign of genocide. In the twelve years of Nazi oppression, upwards of eleven million people were exterminated including 6 million European Jews and millions more non-Jewish Poles, Soviets, Slavs, Romanis, and any other race or class of people deemed a threat to the purity of the master race.[47] Hence, while the level of internal oppression in Stalin's regime was on a par with Hitler's, it was Hitler's stated adherence to the

---

[44] Murphy, *Humanitarian Intervention*, 104.

[45] Litwak, *Rogue States and U.S. Foreign Policy,* 50-52; Barry Rubin, "U.S. Foreign Policy and Rogue States," *Middle East Review of International Affairs* 3, no. 3 (September 1999), http://meria.idc.ac.il/journal/1999/issue3/jv3n3a7.html (accessed 30 January 2008).

[46] Steven Rosefielde, "Incriminating Evidence: Excess Deaths and Forced Labour under Stalin: A Final Reply to Critics," *Soviet Studies* 39, no. 2 (April 1987): 292; Robert Conquest, "Revisioning Stalin's Russia," *Russian Review* 46, no. 4 (October 1987): 388.

[47] United States Holocaust Memorial Museum, "The Holocaust," *Holocaust Encyclopedia,* http://www.ushmm.org/wlc/article.php?lang=en&ModuleId=10005143 (accessed 23 April 2008).

rule of force, and his demonstrated use of force on his neighbors, that won him the scorn of the free world.[48]

This is not to say the world is not concerned when governments oppress their people, but such oppression has rarely been sufficient to lead to isolation as a rogue state. The People's Republic of China (PRC) is a case in point. The PRC has a clearly established history of using its military to suppress human rights yet continues to enjoy healthy relations with its neighbors, a growing economy, and a growing role in the regional affairs of Asian states. Tens of millions of people lost their lives due to oppressive governmental controls in the first thirty years of the PRC's regime, and while conditions in the country have improved since 1978, the PRC still maintains strict controls on personal liberties.[49] The American Department of State's most recent report on the status of human rights in the PRC reports abuses including arbitrary or unlawful deprivation of life, torture, sexual and physical abuse of detained individuals, arbitrary arrest, denial of fair trial, and aggressive tactics to deny or suppress free speech.[50] Further, the PRC's nuclear capability and human rights record led to significant American debate about whether the United States should pursue sanctions to isolate China as a rogue state. In the end, however, the PRC was not deemed worthy of the rogue mantle as the world did not perceive it to be a threat to its neighbors. Clearly, it is not enough to oppress one's own people to garner the label of rogue nation.[51] It seems suppression of human rights is then a supporting argument rather than a key trait of rogue states in the eyes of the world community.

North Korea is perhaps the embodiment of what is commonly accepted as a rogue state. Having been repulsed in its attack of South Korea in 1950, that regime has maintained a clearly

---

[48] Litwak, *Rogue States and U.S. Foreign Policy,* 7, 47; Rubin, "U.S. Foreign Policy and Rogue States."

[49] The Central Intelligence Agency, Factbook, China page, 15 April 2008, https://www.cia.gov/library/publications/the-world-factbook/geos/ch.html (accessed 25 March 2008).

[50] U.S. Department of State, "China Country Report on Human Rights Practices for 2007," http://www.state.gov/g/drl/rls/hrrpt/2007/100518.htm (accessed 23 April 2008).

[51] Litwak, *Rogue States and U.S. Foreign Policy,* 90.

aggressive rhetoric of hostility toward its democratic neighbor ever since. Furthermore, its

bellicose and bizarre behavior has alienated not only western nations but those nations with

whom it shares political ideology. In 1994 North Korea was estimated to have plutonium

sufficient for one or two nuclear weapons. Since then, the regime has assumed a behavioral

posture vacillating between conciliation and provocation while amassing enough plutonium for

upwards of ten weapons. Further, North Korea's 2006 test launch of a long-range ballistic

missile and the detonation of a nuclear device demonstrate its threatening unpredictability.[52]

Consequently, North Korea has been among the most isolated nations in the world resulting in an

impoverished populace and technologically retarded society. In addition to Webster's rogue traits

of isolation, dangerousness and uncontrollability, North Korea embodies those described by

Anthony Lake in pursuing weapons of mass destruction and threatening its neighbors.[53]

In general then, a rogue state is one that is isolated, dedicated to the rule of force,

oppresses its people, disregards international law, and most of all threatens regional or

international security. American Ambassador to the United Nations Richard Holbrooke described

Saddam Hussein's regime in Iraq in just such terms in January 2001:

> "Saddam Hussein's activities continue to be unacceptable and, in my
> view, dangerous to the region and, indeed, to the world… not only because he
> possesses the potential for weapons of mass destruction but because of the very
> nature of his regime… his willingness to be cruel internally is not unique in the
> world, but the combination of that and his willingness to export his problems
> makes him a clear and present danger at all times."[54]

Actions alone, however, may not be sufficient to identify a rogue state as dire

circumstances may necessitate (for example) disregard for international law. In the end, any

---

[52] Michael J. Mazarr, "The Long Road to Pyongyang: A Case Study in Policymaking Without Direction," *Foreign Affairs* 86, no. 5 (September/October 2007): 86, 90.

[53] Rubin, "U.S. Foreign Policy and Rogue States;" Litwak, *Rogue States and U.S. Foreign Policy,* 223-230.

[54] Judy Aita, "Holbrooke: Iraq Will Be a Major UN Issue for Bush Administration," Excerpted from press conference by Richard Holbrooke, outgoing United States Ambassador to the United Nations, 11 January 2001, http://www.usembassy.it/file2001_01/alia/a1011102.htm (accessed 17April 2008).

rogue state definition must be underpinned not just with actions, but motives as well. So to the aforementioned list of rogue-like action is included the rogue's intent to protect or further its interest to the detriment of the greater good. It is within this framework that American behavior is examined throughout the remainder of this paper.

Benevolent Hegemon or Occupying Tyrant?

Given this loose framework of rogue state characteristics, is there a basis for the perception of the United States as a rogue nation? Pundits of the rogue-America rhetoric focus on American military employments as evidence of its dedication to the rule of force. In addition to the apparent pre-eminence of the military in American foreign policy, rogue-America pundits note the United States possesses the world's largest stockpiles of smallpox, anthrax and nuclear weapons.[55] Others are drawn to the imperialist characteristics of the past and present United States. Some of these individuals cite America's hundreds of military installations across the globe as evidence of its roguish imperialism. As Chalmers Johnson observes, the United States stations overseas more military personnel than civilian diplomats and aid workers, "a point not lost on the lands to which they are assigned. Our garrisons send a daily message that the United States prefers to deal with other nations through the use of threat of force rather than negotiations, commerce, or cultural interaction."[56] Of course, the shear power of the United States is sufficient to generate suspicions of its intent on global hegemony. As Samuel Huntington notes, the regional powers will redouble their efforts to achieve multipolarity if they perceive America is intent on achieving unipolarity.[57] Still, the imposing physical stature of the United States is insufficient to ascribe to it the label of rogue state.

---

[55] Jennifer Rankin, "Is America a Rogue State?" *The Foreign Policy Centre*, 2003, http://fpc.org.uk/fsblob/247.pdf (accessed 25 January 2008).

[56] Johnson, *The Sorrows of Empire*, 5.

[57] Huntington, "The Lonely Superpower," 37.

So if there is be a basis for perception of the United States as a rogue state, a corollary question must also be asked: does American foreign policy demonstrate roguish intent? Examining American foreign policy history facilitates answering both questions and, since threatening one's neighbors is perhaps the pre-eminent rogue trait, American military history as well. Further, since humanitarian concerns also drive judgments of rogue behavior, use of American military forces in constabulary roles is of particular interest.

The evolution of American foreign policy in the twentieth century can be viewed as a maturation of Wilsonian ideals into realism underpinned by idealist liberalism… a transition from America as the "city on a hill" as a shining beacon for the world to emulate, to that of crusader imposing America's exceptional values on the rest of the world. Ironically, it was only through the crusader realist approach that the Wilsonian ideal was met. Indeed, America's crusade through the latter half of the twentieth century resulted in the current world order that has as its basis Wilson's fourteen-point idealism.[58]

At the same time, the United States has a long history of expeditionary military employment. From westward continental expansion to American occupation of foreign lands in the early twentieth century, the United States demonstrated a willingness to use its military to achieve even high-minded foreign policy objectives. Further, the United States did not shrink from using these forces to provide governance or assert its will on a conquered populace.

The earliest years of the United States saw a military that was expeditionary in nature. With the exception of brief conventional wars with both the British and Mexicans, the American military spent most of its Antebellum history conducting less conventional missions of coastal defense, protection of American economic interests and frontier law-enforcement. In policing the Nation's frontier, the American Army was tasked to "enforce laws and treaties, explore and

---

[58] Michael Dunne, "Hemisphere and the Globe: the Terms of American Foreign Relations," *International Affairs* 70, no. 4 (October 1994): 704.

govern new territories, punish hostile aggression, and regulate Indian-white contact."[59]

Following the Civil War, the military resumed its expeditionary posture and traditional duties of protecting the frontiers and economic interests. In addition, the Army was tasked with pacification and reconstruction tasks in the occupation of the South and the "Indian question" on the ever-expanding Western frontier. Along with its conventional warfighting skills, the American soldier was called upon to quell labor disputes and maintained "roles of engineer, laborer, policeman, border guard, explorer, administrator, and governor."[60] By 1890, American Army officers were attempting to reverse the trend toward a constabulary army to one of conventional warfighting and national defense. Ironically, however, their efforts were resisted by lawmakers whose memory of the army's "tyranny" and "despotism" in its southern occupation and dealings with America's workers were sufficient to block legislation necessary to retool.[61] Nevertheless, having consolidated all the skills of a constabulary force, the American Army was well postured for the nation building required of its country's forthcoming imperial impulses.

In the aftermath of a short war with Spain in 1898, the United States found itself with stewardship of Cuba, Puerto Rico, and the Philippines and began the era of American imperialism. The military occupation of each of these former colonies was begun with the high-minded ideal of guiding them toward "the fruits of Western… civilization" with an eye toward establishing "self-governing (though perhaps not independent) democratic societies." The Army set about the task of nation-building in its occupied territories with a strategy of self-interested ethics based upon legal doctrines of occupation well entrenched in its institutional knowledge, as well as its constabulary experiences in the post-war South and on the western frontier. The former established the moral obligation of the occupier to provide for the populace while the

---

[59] Andrew J. Birtle, *U.S. Army Counterinsurgency and Contingency Operations Doctrine 1860-1941* (Washington, D.C.: Center of Military History, United States Army, 1998), 7.

[60] Birtle, *U.S. Army Counterinsurgency and Contingency Operations Doctrine,* 55.

[61] Allan R. Millett and Peter Maslowski, *For the Common Defense* (New York: The Free Press, 1984), 248.

latter put into place an informal doctrine of "benevolent paternalism" captured in texts of the Army's officer education.[62]

Back home, the military occupation's strategy in the new territories and its military sponsorship escalated domestic debate on the United States' newfound imperialism. The strategy of self-interested ethics was at odds with American principles of liberty and self-determination and, as discussed later, Americans were ever-suspicious of governance by the military.[63] Ironically, the anti-imperialist concern with forced liberty was concisely articulated by an Army general charged with pacification in the Philippines. In describing the occupation's strategy, Brigadier General Franklin Bell explained "government by force alone cannot be satisfactory to Americans. It is desirable that a government be established in time which is based upon the will of the governed. This can be accomplished satisfactorily only by obtaining and retaining the good will of the people."[64]

Meanwhile, the Army set about erecting the institutions of governance and constructing the infrastructure necessary for building new democratic nations. In building roads, bridges, schools and public facilities, and in establishing municipal governments, the Army was successful in reducing disease, spurring economic growth, and raising the standard of living of the millions of people in the occupied territories. However, American values and methods were difficult to infuse into societies that for so long had functioned in an oligarchic construct under Spanish rule.[65] Indeed, the "veneer of American-style institutions" rapidly disintegrated following the Americans' departure from Cuba in 1902[66], while the strategy's disregard for traditional social

---

[62] Birtle, *U.S. Army Counterinsurgency and Contingency Operations Doctrine*, 99-102.

[63] Birtle, *U.S. Army Counterinsurgency and Contingency Operations Doctrine*, 108.

[64] Ibid., 119.

[65] Millett and Maslowski, *For the Common Defense,* 287, 291.

[66] The deterioration in Cuba became sufficiently acute that President Roosevelt ordered the military to return in 1906 under the terms of the Platt Amendment.

norms created discontent, and ultimately an insurgency for independence in the Philippines.[67] The occupation Army added more repressive pacification techniques to its more benevolent nation building enterprises and as the violence escalated, the Army gradually escalated the severity of its coercion. Inevitably, some soldiers committed atrocities, and though these were few, their impact served to fuel the anti-imperialist debate in the United States. This in turn served the insurgents' propaganda agenda which further emboldened the insurgency. As one American officer observed, "every disloyal sentiment uttered by a man of prominence in the United States is repeatedly broadcast through the islands and greatly magnified." Thus emboldened, insurgents escalated their violence which increased soldier frustration and, hence, led to more brutal tactics on the part of the Army.[68]

Though the counterinsurgency eventually won out, the Philippines remained under Army occupation until 1913, and the realities of the brutality required to win the peace bore a heavy toll on many American military men. The occupation strategy had been an idealist amalgam of "enlightened self-interest, historical precedent, genuine humanity, progressive reform impulses, and traditional American ideals," but it was "decisive military action and the policies of chastisement" that were key to the successful counterinsurgency.[69] In the words of one Army general the United States had "ruthlessly suppressed in the Philippines an insurrection better justified than was our Revolution of glorious memory."[70]

As mentioned earlier, the founders of the new American republic were also deeply suspicious of standing armies. Many state constitutions at the time contained language that

[67] Birtle, *U.S. Army Counterinsurgency and Contingency Operations Doctrine*, 106; Millett and Maslowski, *For the Common Defense,* 289.

[68] Birtle, *U.S. Army Counterinsurgency and Contingency Operations Doctrine*, 26-134; Millett and Maslowski, *For the Common Defense,* 291-292.

[69] Birtle, *U.S. Army Counterinsurgency and Contingency Operations Doctrine*, 119, 135.

[70] Millett and Maslowski, *For the Common Defense,* 296.

cautioned "standing armies are dangerous to liberty."[71] The aversion to standing armies was no doubt influenced by the recency of America's experience under colonial rule. By spring 1770, the British empire was asserting its authority over the colonies through a military presence to extract additional taxes. On the 5th of May a crowd of jeering colonists was fired upon by a group of British soldiers outside the Boston Customs House. Five people were killed and the Boston Massacre became a rallying cry for American independence from tyranny and oppression.[72] The resultant constitution distributed powers such that the authority of commanding the nation's army was bestowed on the president, but the authority to declare war, raise and sustain an army was conferred upon the legislature. This separation of powers was specifically intended to avert the use of the Nation's army as an instrument of oppression.

Perhaps the closest an American standing army came to realizing this concern came in 1932. In June of that year, twelve thousand World War I veterans marched on Washington in an effort to influence Congress to accelerate maturity of bonds awarded them as a bonus for their service. When the measure was blocked in the Senate, the so-called Bonus Expeditionary Force rioted and had to be suppressed by an active duty Army regiment. Several people were killed and hundreds injured as a result of the riot raising concern on the appropriateness of using the Army to compel law and order on American citizens.[73] Indeed, perception of armies as instruments of oppression continue to be relevant in today's environment where the military has such a prominent role in American foreign policy.

Against the backdrop of American expeditionary ventures and perception of the military as tools of tyrants, American foreign policy became increasingly militaristic after the Cold War. Even as parts of the world regarded militaries with suspicion, and having spent the better part of

---

[71] Alexander Hamilton, *The Federalist Papers* (New York: Bantam Books, 1982), 117.

[72] The Library of Congress, "America's Story: Boston Massacre," *America's Library,* http://www.americaslibrary.gov/cgi-bin/page.cgi/jb/revolut/boston_1.

[73] John W. Killigrew, "The Army and the Bonus Incident," *Military Affairs* 26, no. 2 (Summer 1962).

the twentieth century focused on preparing for major theater war, the American military found itself in ever-expanding roles and missions toward the end of the twentieth century. American foreign policy, however, was problematic in that it was poorly defined and constantly changing. In the absence of a coherent National strategy, the American military, as an instrument capable of quick action, was increasingly called upon to execute missions other than war as a primary means of demonstrating National resolve, even if policy guidance was vague or lacking. Indeed, uncertainty in how America should proceed in the face of failures in diplomacy and economic sanctions led to American military involvement in Somalia, Haiti, and Bosnia in the 1990s. [74] Further, that same policy incoherence resulted in those operations evolving from humanitarian provisioning and/or peacekeeping, to law enforcement or nation-building activities for which the military was ill prepared. Well after American forces landed in Somalia with a mission of ensuring distribution of humanitarian aid, American Secretary of State Warren Christopher declared "for the first time there will be a sturdy American role to… rebuild a viable nation state."[75]

The United States government became more reliant on military options as the military expanded its readiness to accomplish the myriad new missions it was called upon to execute. The resulting mission creep created a downward spiral of over reliance on the military instrument of National power: as America increasingly called on its military to accomplish foreign policy objectives, the military services expended time and resources to prepare for and execute them, effectively expanding military mission sets and broadening future military employment options. Simultaneously, the military was enduring peace dividend budget cuts and the other instruments of National power withered from under- use. Indeed, this period was arguably most frustrating to

---

[74] Linda B. Miller, "The Clinton Years: Reinventing US Foreign Policy," *International Affairs* 70, no. 4 (October 1994): 626-629.

[75] Herspring, *The Pentagon and the Presidency*, 344.

a military that "may not want to send forces to Somalia, Bosnia, or Kosovo, but if the order comes it wants to know what it is supposed to do."[76]

The American military initially viewed operations such as peacekeeping, law enforcement and nation-building as the temporary excursions of an American administration obliged to "build a multinational community by providing military forces when necessary."[77] Only after repeated operations did the American military begin to develop doctrine for their emergent missions. Starting with "low intensity conflict" (LIC) doctrine in 1990, the military establishment attempted to keep pace with the rapid, ever-expanding roles and missions with which it was tasked. As missions accrued over the next ten years, low-intensity conflict doctrine evolved into "military operations other than war," followed by "full-spectrum operations," and finally into military operations as a "seamless combination of offense, defense, stability, and support."[78]

Still, the growth in missions outpaced the ability of civilian leaders to adequately direct preparation for them, so in November 2005 the Secretary of Defense implemented a new department-wide directive that instructed "U.S. military forces shall be prepared to perform all tasks necessary to establish or maintain order when civilians cannot do so" to include being ready to "build the private sector, including encouraging citizen-driven, bottom-up economic activity and constructing necessary infrastructure."[79] Many tactical-level commanders were conducting just such activities shortly after the invasion of Iraq in 2003, recognizing these as essential to furthering the stability of Iraq. Indeed, among the first major moves following the Defense Secretary's November 2005 directive, Deputy Secretary of Defense Gordon England established the Task Force for Business and Stability Operations (TFBSO) in Iraq. Manned primarily with

---

[76] Herspring, *The Pentagon and the Presidency*, 36, 374.

[77] Ibid., 338.

[78] Thomas Ricks, *Fiasco* (New York: Penguin Books, 2007), 152.

[79] U.S. Department of Defense. Directive 3000.05, "Military Support for Stability, Security, Transition, and Reconstruction (SSTR) Operations," 28 November 2005 (Washington, D.C.), 2.

leaders and analysts from the international business and manufacturing community, the TFBSO is tasked with "revitalizing the Iraqi economy and reducing the rampant unemployment of the Iraqi population — a significant factor that fuels the insurgency."[80]

American foreign policy in the post 9-11 environment further complemented the perception of America as a rogue state in its seeming dedication to the rule of force. The United States employed overwhelming force to successfully accomplish military objectives in Afghanistan and Iraq in pursuit of National goals. Without, however, the muscular employment of non-military instruments in the aftermath of these conflicts, America appeared indifferent to its stated intent to "actively work to bring the hope of democracy, development, free markets, and free trade to every corner of the world."[81]

Playing Rough with Rogues: the Paradox of Hussein's Iraq

Saddam Hussein's Iraq represents the ultimate dilemma posed by the use of force on rogue states. On the one hand, the United States exercised over a decade of soft power in attempts to eliminate the threat Iraq posed to its neighbors and the world order. But when all indications were that Iraq was attempting to build an arsenal of nuclear weapons, the United States felt armed force was imperative to avert the nuclear threat and eliminate the rogue state. Saddam Hussein encouraged the perception of its intent to build a nuclear arsenal as a means of preserving his power and perpetuate the rogue state. But Hussein's deception miscalculated the American response and led to the demise of his rogue regime.[82]

With synchronization and joint cooperation unprecedented in military history, the United States led a coalition that routed the Iraqi army and overthrew the regime of Saddam Hussein in a

---

[80] Paul Brinkley, "A Cause for Hope: Economic Revitalization in Iraq," *Military Review* 87, no. 4 (July-August 2007): 2-11.

[81] President. *The National Security Strategy of the United States of America* (September 2002): 2.

[82] Washington Post. "Hussein Mistook American Intentions," *Kansas City Star,* (27 January 2008), A20.

matter of mere weeks. Having commenced combat operations on the 20th of March, by 1 May the President of the United States declared the Iraq operation had been "carried out with a combination of precision and speed and boldness the enemy did not expect, and the world had not seen before."[83]

By the summer of 2003, the glow of a liberated Iraq soon turned to growing suspicion: large caches of weapons of mass destruction were nowhere to be found, de-Baathification eviscerated government enterprises, and the coalition occupation began to draw comparisons with the colonialization so prevalent in the area's history. While the vast majority of American soldiers wholly believed in the benevolent nature of their mission, Iraqis equated the American occupation with the Hun invasion of Iraq in 1258 saying the Americans "want to wipe out our culture." To wit, American soldiers viewed their visit to a school for disadvantaged children as a gesture of encouragement, while the school's neighbors suggested "only God knows" what nefarious activity was happening inside the school.[84] In the absence of a functioning government, these constabulary forces provided rudimentary governance even while attempting to maintain security. America's intentions, no matter how benevolent, were looked upon with increasing suspicion as the occupations dragged on without any sign of indigenous governance.[85] Hence, the paradoxical turn of the position of the United States from protector of world order to roguish threat to peace and stability.

Trends in Rogue America Perception

As mentioned in the introduction, there are currently two trends toward global perception of a rogue America: one toward isolation from other participants in the current world order; and

---

[83] George W. Bush, Speech from the USS Abraham Lincoln, 1 May 2003, http://www.whitehouse.gov/news/releases/2003/05/20030501-15.html (accessed 21 January 2008).

[84] Ricks, *Fiasco,* 152-153, 178.

[85] Ibid., 152-153, 176-178.

the other of emerging powers exploiting rogue America rhetoric to advance their own power ambitions.

The first of these trends is perhaps the most volatile should it run a course leading to American isolation. While no sovereign governments in the free world have yet adopted rogue-America rhetoric, there have been public overtures of increased displeasure with American foreign policy. In an interview on Dutch television in April 2004, former Dutch Prime Minister Dries Van Agt recommended the Dutch government withdraw its troops from Iraq characterizing the effort as illegal occupation without a United Nations mandate. He went on to condemn American support to Israel as "irresponsible and unjust," and called the United States a "rogue state" for repeatedly ignoring international law.[86] Additionally, the communist parties in Italy, Norway and Canada have all accused the United States of rogue behavior.[87] In the aftermath of NATO's military intervention in Kosovo, the Executive Director of France's leading think tank cautioned the United States "could become an isolated country" and wrote "the United States could itself qualify for the category" of rogue state due to its "turning away from international institutions, an increase in unilateral and coercive practices, a disdain for legality, and more generally a growing reluctance to tolerate any international constraints."[88] And, in 2006, Britain's Royal Institute of International Affairs published an analysis of Iran in which the Iranian government's erratic behavior was compared with that of the United States warning "the danger lies in the risk that Ahmadinejad's confrontational politics will… become even more unshackled in ambition and, in mirroring those of his neo-conservative rivals in the U.S., engage in a provocation too far."[89]

---

[86] Nova Television, "Former Dutch PM Wants Iraq Pull-Out," *Al Jazeera,* 27 April 2004, http://english.aljazeera.net/English/Archive/Archive?ArchiveID=3340 (accessed 19 September 2007).

[87] Korean Central News Agency, "U.S. Termed Facist and Rogue State," 8 March 2003, http://www.globalsecurity.org/wmd/library/news/dprk/2003/dprk-030310-kcna06.htm (accessed 16 November 2007).

[88] Boniface, "Reflections on America As A World Power," 10, 15.

[89] Robert Lowe and Claire Spencer, "Iran, Its Neighbours and the Regional Crises," Chatham

Typically, however, the language of these missives is more cautionary than confrontational, being largely more critical of segments of American thought (e.g. neoconservatism) than American foreign policy in general. Indeed, many times anti-American missives are also accompanied by language praising United States leadership. For example, in the same 2003 speech in which the foreign minister of the European Union warned how American national interests could come to be at odds with the world order, Chris Patten made clear this was not yet the case in praising American multilateralism especially in working through the United Nations to seek resolution of the looming crisis in Iraq.[90] A year later, Mr Patten reiterated America's "global leadership" and reminded "there is so much more that unites than divides" Americans and Europeans.[91] In fact, far from offering blanket condemnation of American foreign policy, each European Union Commissioner for External Relations from 9/11 to present has called upon European nations to accept a greater role in regional and global security efforts rather than leaving the burden on the United States by offering "bromides and cop-outs."[92] In September 2007, the commissioner re-affirmed European commitment to sharing the security burden emphasizing "as the EU strengthens its foreign policy role... the US will find us an ever more willing and able partner; better equipped to take an even greater share of the diplomatic, aid and military burden."[93] Hence, while America's friends and allies may sometimes be critical of its foreign policy, they are far from calling for its isolation as a rogue nation.

House (The Royal Institute of International Affairs), 2006, 8.

[90] Patten, Oxford, 30 January 2003.

[91] Chris Patten, "Europe and America: Has the Transatlantic Relationship Run Out of Road?" (lecture, Lady Margaret Hall, Oxford, 13 February 2004), http://ec.europa.eu/external_relations/news/patten/sp04_77.htm (accessed 24 January 2008).

[92] Ibid.

[93] Ferrero-Waldner, "Opportunities and Challenges in the EU-US Relationship," 28 September 2007.

More prevalent (yet more insidious) is the trend of emerging powers exploiting rogue-America rhetoric to promote an alternative regional or world order. Venezuela, Iran, Russia, and China all demonstrate this behavior. Iran, China and Russia are archetypes of this second trend, employing generalized rogue-America rhetoric without citing specific grievances as a means of strumming a chord that quickly achieves a highly resonant excitation as a way to generate support for their own, unstated self-interested behavior. Non-state actors also exploit rogue-America rhetoric to advance their agendas as evidenced by Al Qaeda and Jemaah Islamiyah.

In the Middle East, America's military operations in Afghanistan and Iraq have heightened Southwest Asian suspicions of American motives in the Middle East. Among America's top rogues, Iran is threatened by American militarism and "crises unleashed or aggravated through Western military interventions," and the proliferation of American military installations in the region adds to their concern.[94] At an Arab summit in Saudi Arabia in March 2007, Saudi King Abdullah condemned the "illegal, foreign occupation" of Iraq.[95]

Iran continues to cite American support to the government of the former shah of Iran as an example of contradictory American foreign policy: the United States emphasizes the primacy of democracy and human rights yet supported, and continues to support less-than-democratic regimes with poor human rights records.[96] Iran also cites America's support to the state of Israel as further evidence of roguish American intent in supporting Israel's terrorism against the Palestinians and Lebanese in contradiction to its foreign policy abhorring terrorism and those regimes that facilitate it.[97] Iran continues to emphasize these apparent contradictions as a means of driving a wedge between the United States and other nations in the Middle East.

---

[94] Lowe and Spencer, "Iran, Its Neighbours and the Regional Crises," 8.

[95] Henderson, "Saudi Arabia: the Nightmare of Iraq," 36.

[96] For more on the hypocrisy of American foreign policy, see Carl Boggs' *Masters of War*. The book proposes America's propensity for force and support to less than democratic regimes will generate world resentment and eventual retaliation.

[97] President. *The National Security Strategy of the United States of America* (March 2006): 3.

This trend in the Middle East is advancing even among more moderate voices in the Arab world. By some, the invasion of Iraq is viewed as a threat to world order in meddling in other states' internal affairs and unfettered dedication to the rule of force. Gamil Matar, an acclaimed Egyptian scholar and moderate, and proponent for democracy in the Middle East, noted with frustration in 2006: "When Washington turns a blind eye to the anti-democratic behavior of some of its allies while lashing out at other countries for the same sins, one cannot avoid the conclusion that Washington is manipulating the appeal to democracy for its own ends."[98]

China also uses rogue-America rhetoric to advance its own agenda. In 1997, the People's Republic of China (PRC) unveiled a "New Security Concept" as an alternative to the current world order. Within the PRC's rhetoric to support such an alternative is the claim that American policies are a significant cause of instability throughout the world. This claim is consistently reinforced in PRC rhetoric in defense of the New Security Concept. For example, in language clearly directed at the United States, the PRC's 2000 Defense White Paper asserted the current world order was dominated by "certain big powers pursuing 'neo-interventionism,' new 'gunboat policy' and neo-economic colonialism, which are seriously damaging the sovereignty, independence and development interests of many countries, and threatening world peace and security."[99] Subsequent to the New Security Concept's introduction, China has risen to unprecedented influence in Asian affairs including interaction with, and expansion of the Association of Southeast Asian Nations, Shanghai Cooperation Organization, increased investment throughout the region, and China is leading development of the East Asia Community, an economic and political organization similar to the European Union.[100]

---

[98] Gamil Matar, "A Marriage Made in Hell," *Al Ahram Weekly,* 5 April 2006, http://weekly.ahram.org.eg/2006/788/op2.htm (accessed 19 January 2008).

[99] Denny Roy, "China's Pitch for a Multipolar World," *Asia-Pacific Center for Security Studies* 2, no. 1 (May 2003): 2.

[100] Jin H. Pak, "China's Pragmatic Rise: and U.S. Interests in East Asia," *Military Review* 87, no. 6 (November-December 2007): 56-68.

Russia also employs rogue-America rhetoric to support a new world order. In its January 2000 National Security Blueprint, Russia maintains American hegemony and its dominance of NATO are causal in most of its national security problems. The document maintains the current international relations structure is at odds with Russian interests as it is a United States-dominated system "designed for unilateral solutions (including the use of military force) to key issues in world politics in circumvention of the fundamental rules of international law." The document goes on to add "military force and violence remain substantial aspects of international relations" and that unilateral actions by American-led NATO "could destabilize the entire global strategic situation. In short, American unilateralism and propensity for use of force make violent conflict inevitable. Russia proposes to lead development of a new ideology based on multipolarity. Ignoring the obvious contradiction between leadership and multipolarity, it is sufficient to understand Russia feels itself vulnerable and wishes to marginalize America's global influence.[101]

The effectiveness of this trend is evident in Africa. Suspicious of "predatory" American intent, the regional powers of Nigeria, South Africa, Algeria, Libya, Morocco and the fourteen-country Southern African Development Community collectively refused to allow basing America's new African geographic command headquarters in their countries. Concern is so grave, the South African defense minister cautioned the presence of the American headquarters would not encourage a "sense of security."[102] The effectiveness of rogue-America rhetoric is most evident, however, in the Middle East where such rhetoric exploits a collective memory of recent imperial occupations of the Ottoman and British empires to foment dissent and weaken American ties to the region. In an address to the Los Angeles World Affairs Council, former

---

[101] The Russian Federation, "National Security Blueprint," January 2000, as translated by the U.S. Foreign Broadcast Information Service and excerpted in *Arms Control Today,* January/February 2000, http://www.armscontrol.org/act/2000_01-02/docjf00.asp (accessed 23 January 2008).

[102] Sean McFate, "U.S. Africa Command: A New Strategic Paradigm," *Military Review* (January-February 2008), 18-19.

Arab League Ambassador to the United Nations Clovis Maksoud advised Arabs must "unlearn [the] distortions the enemies of the United States have inflicted upon us."[103]

Lastly, quantitative data supports the conclusion American foreign policy is diverging from the rest of the world. Political scientist Erik Voeten analyzed the votes of one-hundred fifty-four countries during 283 roll calls from 1991 to 2001on 75 United Nations resolutions on issues pertaining to the Middle East, security, human rights, sanctions of other nations. The results depicted in figure 1 clearly show a trend of major power votes diverging from those of the United States. Mr Voeten attributes this "preference gap" to the demise of the Soviet Union which unified Western powers and increased American unilateralism since the mid 1990s.[104] He concludes "U.S. hegemony has elicited almost universal resistance" and the United States "finds itself increasingly isolated in multilateral organizations."

[103] Clovis Maksoud, "The Future of Arab-U.S. Relations: Problems and Prospects," speech to the Los Angeles World Affairs Council, 20 September 2007, 5, http://www.lawac.org/speech/indexes/2007-08_index.htm (accessed 19 December 2007).

[104] Erik Voeten, "Resisting the Lonely Superpower: Responses of States in the United Nations to U.S. Dominance," *The Journal of Politics* 66, no. 3 (August 2004): 729-754.

Countering Rogue America Rhetoric

The rogue-America rhetoric persists because American foreign policy actions have become increasingly militaristic but its strategic communications have not adequately conveyed the intent of those actions. Because American motives are misunderstood, however, there is no reason the United States government should disregard such rhetoric. On the contrary, should the rogue-America discourse migrate from fringe elements and academia to think-tanks or national policy-making bodies, American foreign policy would be adversely affected. It is conceivable the rogue view could then become the official position of other nations in the free world, and, with enough international support, the United States could eventually become isolated from the world community.

Much like the rhetoric of states exploiting rogue-America rhetoric for their own purposes, intellectual elites like Chalmers Johnson, Noam Chomsky and William Blum support their rogue-

---

[105] Voeten, "Resisting the Lonely Superpower," (August 2004): 742.

America thesis without specific fact, but with sweeping generalities. Citing corruption, human rights abuses, and personal liberty violations, these individuals skillfully employ the high-minded language of America's democratic ideals to substantiate their argument. The United States government has typically taken a high-ground approach to these missives by dismissing them outright. However, that these outbursts have proliferated should concern the American government as the rogue America argument could gain traction in policy-making circles simply through the shear volume of the public articles.

As noted earlier, the United States will continue to employ its military to conduct operations other than war in accordance with the Defense Department's 2005 directive,[106] and the world will continue to challenge America's rationale for doing so. Hence, the United States must be prepared to demonstrate its benevolent intent in concise and sustained words, and support these through transparent and carefully planned action.

Emphasis on Globalization.

Just as education is crucial to successful democratization, it is equally imperative in furthering globalization. Education themes should focus on globalization as an inclusive, not exclusive, phenomenon. There are no big winners, or losers with globalization; only those whom remain outside the globalized system stand to lose. As the largest partner in the global economic order, the United States must embrace its role as protector and promoter of globalization.[107]

However, the United States as protector of a global system puts it in a position of seemingly roguish behavior. Many see globalization as the motive (self-interest) of American global hegemony and an unrivaled military as the means. With this logic American foreign policy actions are merely opportunities to advance American imperialism to perpetuate the globalist world order it created. The fundamental flaw in this line of thought is that in advancing

---

[106] U.S. Department of Defense. Directive 3000.05, 28 November 2005.

[107] Freidman, *Lexus and the Olive Tree,* 372.

globalism one is advancing a system in which any nation can participate and succeed, not one of past imperialism in which the many are exploited by the few. Further, global economics has always been a prominent part of American foreign policy interests. As foreign policy analyst Walter Russell Mead observes, "the chief international concern of the American people through the centuries has been the relationship of the United States to the growing and changing global economic and political order."[108] Indeed, globalism is merely an instrument for advancing the liberal democratic ideals of building a free-market environment in which individuals are afforded liberty to pursue personal opportunity. Whole societies of so-liberated individuals creates conditions favorable for the "autonomous choice" necessary for liberal democracy to succeed.[109]

Trade deficits and the level of interdependence of the global economy are also points which refute the assertion the United States seeks to fence economic opportunity exclusively for Americans. The current global dynamic is one in which all its participants are stakeholders, rather than one in which only imperial powers have a stake. As shown earlier, the 1997 global market downturn, or the January 2008 American credit squeeze demonstrate the inextricable interconnectedness of globalism. These are merely two of many examples of how the fortunes of all participants in globalization are inextricably dependent.

Globalism has also created trade deficits where the "powerful" nations absorb goods from lesser nations as a means of jump-starting those nations' integration into the global economy. What, then, is the interest of powerful nations in furthering globalization? Quite simply, it is to promote global security through democratization and good governance. As more nations

---

[108] Walter Russell Mead, *Special Providence: American Foreign Policy and How it Changed the World* (New York: Routledge, 2002), 313.

[109] Francis Fukuyama, *The End of History and the Last Man Standing.* (New York:Perennial, 2002), 205-206; Michael Mandelbaum, "Democracy Without America: the Spontaneous Spread of Freedom," *Foreign Affairs* 86, no. 5 (September/October 2007): 123-124.

embrace the liberating aspects of globalization, the tenets of democracy continue to spread. Therefore, as global economic competition spreads, violent competition declines.[110]

America's millennium challenge account is just such a vehicle for advancing positive change. Currently limited to political reform and governance criteria, the millennium challenge criteria should be expanded to link foreign aid to integration with the global economy. Further, some of this aid should be structured to advance the recipient counties capacity for self-sustained interstate economic participation.[111] So rather than assistance based solely on measures of democratic reforms, the American government would be compelling these reforms through participation in a free market which is the foundation of democracies around the world.

Lastly, the United States should emphasize American military presence as a means to ensure equal access for all in the global economy. The long period of relative peace in the Asia-Pacific region has been accompanied by a period of unprecedented economic growth. That peace and prosperity are directly resultant from America's leadership in fostering the region's security is a story that is largely lost on the world today. The United States should emphasize this point when discussions of American military forward presence emerge in public discourse. This leads to the next area requiring attention by the American government.

Reinvigorate Strategic Communications

In an address to the United Nations in 1993, American President Bill Clinton proclaimed "the United States would act multilaterally when possible, but unilaterally when necessary."[112] On the surface this would seem to be the position of an arrogant nation unconcerned with the strictures of international norms. But this ignores the events of the time which saw the rising tide of violence in the Balkans as a threat to the security of Eurasia. Furthermore, American

---

[110] Thomas L. Friedman, *The World Is Flat* (New York: Farrar, Straus and Giroux, 2005), 103-113, 461-464.

[111] George Soros, *The Bubble of American Supremacy* (New York: Public Affairs, 2004), 128.

[112] Chomsky, *Rogue States,* 4.

leadership in the Balkans accomplished what Europe and Russia alone could not: averting debilitating civil war, genocide, and the emergence of Serbia as a new rogue nation.[113] Yet, to this day President Clinton's quote is used as evidence of America's roguish foreign policy.

The United States government consistently fails to articulate its National intent when employing its military, especially in situations where the military is not the government's main effort (e.g. stability and reconstruction operations). Large portions of the world's population equate military action with aggression and oppression. Yet, America's strategic communications have not risen to a level sufficient to dispel global perceptions that its actions are neither tyrannical nor imperialist in intent. As Walter Mead observes, American engagement with the world is "incoherent, contradictory, and ultimately less effective than it needs to be."[114] Given America's reliance on its military to carry out foreign policy objectives throughout the spectrum of conflict, it is imperative the United States government do more to bridge its National Security Strategy with operational necessities through consistent and sustained strategic communications.

Just as military strategists have employed indirect approaches to military campaigns, the United States government should adopt less direct foreign policy statements in those areas where its policy may be seen as contradictory to its friends and allies in the region. Such a strategy in foreign policy would be more compatible with nonwestern cultures where the inherent directness of western culture is not well understood.[115] In the Far East, for example, western directness is in many cases offensive or denigrating, and as Joseph Nye notes "our presence in the [Persian] Gulf could be handled more subtly."[116] Furthermore, America's strategic communications are complicated by popular opinion in foreign nations and must take into account the relationship

---

[113] Richard Holbrooke, *To End a War* (New York: The Modern Library, 1999), 21-33.

[114] Mead, *Special Providence,* 322.

[115] Richard Halloran, "Strategic Communication," *Parameters* 37, no 3, (Autumn 2007): 9.

[116] Nye, *Paradox of American Power,* 144.

between governments and their populace. This is especially important in those regions of the world where "saving face" is an imperative to the success of any endeavor.

A case in point for both these dynamics is Pakistan's January 2008 general elections. While Pakistanis are largely hostile toward American influence in Pakistan's affairs, they generally do not acknowledge America's role in pressuring Pervez Musharaf for free and fair elections in Pakistan. [117] The ensuing euphoria of the Pakistani populace is a positive result of American influence largely lost on Pakistanis and the rest of the world. While some print journalists in Pakistan acknowledged America's positive influence, the effectiveness of these communications is of limited effectiveness due to Pakistan's fifty percent rate of literacy.[118] Hence, America's strategic communications must accommodate governments whose association with the United States may strain their relationship with their respective populaces.

Others propose actions that are counterproductive in countering the rogue rhetoric and repairing America's relations with the world. George Soros, for example, recommends the United States undermine the role of African nations by taking a lead role in the affairs of the African Union. Soros also advocates pushing the Association of Southeast Asian States to take a more active role in the internal affairs of member nations.[119] As a member of neither organization, such actions would certainly be met with condemnation of the world community, undermine America's position as the beacon of state self-determination, and would advance the case for America as a rogue state.

Publicly funded American media enterprises should be compelled to broadcast periodic missives on American foreign policy, be they the President's weekly radio address, significant

---

[117] Moeed Pirzada, "Post Election Fault Lines," *Khaleej Times,* 28 Febrary 2008, http://www.khaleejtimes.com/DisplayArticleNew.asp?section=opinion&xfile=data/opinion/2008/february/opinion_february108.xml (accessed 25 March 2008).

[118] The Central Intelligence Agency, Factbook, Pakistan page, 20 March 2008, https://www.cia.gov/library/publications/the-world-factbook/geos/pk.html#People (accessed 25 March 2008).

[119] Soros, *Bubble of American Supremacy*, 121.

foreign policy decisions, or news of American foreign policy actions. Good news does not sell, therefore, it is unreasonable to expect commercial media ventures to convey American strategic communications. As Richard Lambert notes in research for Harvard's Kennedy School of Government "skewed media representation further shapes and entrenches negative attitudes," and media mogul Rupert Murdock acknowledges the media is too often "motivated by personal gain."[120] However, it is not unreasonable to expect publicly funded media outlets to broadcast America's message. Yet, in a poll by the author of over twenty radio stations in the Saint Louis and Kansas City metropolitan areas, not a single publicly funded or talk-radio station broadcasts the President's weekly address.[121] Publicly funded media should be compelled to do so if they will not voluntarily.

The United States should also be more considerate of how its choice of words affects its foreign policy implementation. Operations in Afghanistan and Iraq continue to be characterized as "wars" by both the American government and the media, when in reality they are post-war stability and reconstruction efforts. Hence, the global focus on these campaigns is conflict rather than the nation-building activities that are at the center of the effort. Ironically, even the nation-building aspects of these campaigns are led by military personnel. With such overwhelming military presence and a focus on conflict, it is no wonder there is a lingering perception the United States places a premium on the use of force, and nation-building achievements are largely ignored.

America's foreign policy critics note the United States contributes just 0.16 percent of its National wealth to foreign aid, ranking number twenty-two among global donors. However, this obscures the impact of American aid in terms of real dollars. In 2004, with just four percent of

---

[120] Ralph D. Berenger, ed., *Global Media Go To War: Role of News and Entertainment Media During the 2003 Iraq War* (Spokane: Marquette Books, 2004), 5, 174. Mr Berenger proposes corporate media inhibit objective news reporting. Ironically, however, he reveals journalists as the true obstacle to objective reporting in dedicating his book (in part) "to journalists everywhere who bare their souls in every story."

[121] Email poll by author to radio stations from December 2007 to March 2008.

the world's population, the United States' 19 billion dollars led all other contributors, providing over 24 percent of the total world contribution and exceeding the second leading donor nation by 114 percent.[122] To this, in 2007, George Bush garnered an additional fifteen billion dollars for his President's Emergency Plan for AIDS Relief (PEPFAR), raising America's total commitment to the initiative to 48.3 billion dollars, and making PEPFAR the largest single-disease effort in history.[123] American strategic communications have failed if these data are not visible to the world community.

The United States should drop the rogue rhetoric from its foreign policy. The language has never resonated with the world community, has limited effectiveness in isolating rogues through diplomacy or sanctions, garners little international support, and limits nuanced foreign policy approaches when dealing with individual states (e.g. diplomacy with China but not Iran is inconsistent with rogue-state dogma).[124] Further, rogue states use their pariah status as a means of garnering international sympathy or, as noted earlier, they adopt the rogue lexicon and turn it back on the United States as a means of redirecting international scorn. Eventually, this "David and Goliath" bravado emboldens rogues to "eschew compromise and engage in high-risk behavior."[125]

Finally, the United States should establish a single entity with responsibility for coordinating and promulgating America's strategic message. A single, overarching strategic communications authority would break through departmental stovepipes to ensure consistency of the administration's message. Such an entity should have authority sufficient to direct expedient

---

[122] Larry Nowels, "Foreign Aid: Understanding Data Used to Compare Donors," CRS Report for Congress, 23 May 2005, 4-5.

[123] Office of National AIDS Policy. "President's HIV/AIDS Initiatives," The White House, http://www.whitehouse.gov/infocus/hivaids (accessed 28 April 2008).

[124] Michael J. Mazarr, "The Long Road to Pyongyang: A Case Study in Policymaking Without Direction," *Foreign Affairs* 86, no. 5 (September/October 2007): 90-91.

[125] Michael Klare, *Rogue States and Nuclear Outlaws: America's Search for a New Foreign Policy* (New York: Hill and Wang, 1995), 219.

action from individual department communications operations centers to facilitate rapid American communications in response to emerging world events. Ideally, this would allow an American government response within the same news cycle as the event itself. The message could then be refined and reiterated in subsequent news cycles.[126]

Regardless of how America's message is conveyed, American motives should be given primacy in all strategic communications. Far from the vague, over-arching rhetoric commonly associated with American foreign policy positions, American motives should be concise and tailored to every situation. Further, American actions should complement, rather than contradict its foreign policy message. This is especially important when employing military forces for benevolent purposes.

Foreign Policy Balance

The United States is in dire need of a more balanced application of power in foreign policy application. This can be achieved through a more cautious approach to military employment and renewed leadership in multilateralism.

Cautious Military Employment

First and foremost, American leaders need an appetite suppressant in the use of military power. Leaders of the United States must remain cognizant that American military actions will almost always be perceived as forays to advance its "aggressive imperialist mission" for the foreseeable future.[127] But American leaders cannot take a military appetite suppressant unless they have other alternatives upon which to draw to advance American interests. Hence, the United States should start now to build the capabilities necessary to expand its non-military

---

[126] Brigadier General Mari K. Eder "Toward Strategic Communication," *Military Review* 87, no. 4 (July-August 2007): 63-64; Halloran, "Strategic Communication," 13.

[127] Madeleine Bunting, "Beginning of the End," *Guardian* (3 February 2003), http://www.guardian.co.uk/world/2003/feb/03/usa.comment (accessed 22 February 2008).

foreign policy options. Further, American lawmakers must become proactive in this regard and work with the Executive to craft and fund new capabilities. In the words of Joseph Nye on the disparity between the Defense and State Department budgets, "our military strength is important, but it is not sixteen times more important than our diplomacy."[128] Even Secretary of Defense Robert Gates highlighted America's overreliance on military power when he commented in November 2007 the United States "must strengthen other important elements of national power both institutionally and financially."[129]

But it is not enough to boost funding to other elements of the Executive without a radical change to institutional paradigms. For example, building an expeditionary arm of the State Department to support other nations in building good governance abroad will only be effective if State Department employees are compelled to deploy regardless of their personal preference. In January of 2008, Secretary of State Condoleezza Rice narrowly averted a mutiny of foreign service officers (FSOs) when it appeared she may have to non-voluntarily reassign some of them to badly needed positions in Iraq. At a meeting on the subject, FSOs signaled with sustained applause their solidarity in opposing the measure when one diplomat stated "it's one thing if someone believes in what's going on over there and volunteers, but it's another thing to send someone over there on a forced assignment."[130] Clearly, the institutional paradigm at the State Department suggests American foreign policy initiatives will get done only if there are sufficient volunteers to get them done. Hence, building new capacity in the State Department is not enough, and any measures to improve America's ability to project other instruments of power must be accompanied by legislation that makes their implementation impervious to institutional norms.

---

[128] Nye, *Paradox of American Power,* 143.

[129] Robert M. Gates. (Landon Lecture, Kansas State University, 26 November 2007), http://www.america.gov/st/texttrans-english/2007/November/20071206191908bpuh0.9181177.html (accessed 21 February 2008).

[130] Associated Press, "U.S. Diplomats in Uproar," *Kansas City Star,* 1 November 2007, A11.

For their part, American military leaders at all levels must remain cognizant of possible negative effects produced by military action and provide reasoned dissent to its chain of command when such action is contemplated. This, in turn, will ensure America's civilian leadership fully understands what will emerge in the wake of military force. The observation that "military leaders must be prepared to assist in accurately estimating the consequences of the threat or use of force against the potentials for persuasion and conflict resolution" are as relevant today as when they were penned at the height of the Cold War.[131] Far from espousing a constabulary military, this is simply and initiative to enhance existing political-military affairs instruction in officer education programs.

The American military must also resist building expedient capability wherever it sees a gap. This behavior, while laudable, often creates larger long-term problems in the interests of advancing American foreign policy objectives in the near term. Ad hoc interagency cells are a case in point. Most every unified combatant commander has an interagency working group or task force for the purpose of synchronizing with other instruments of National power in the interests of ensuring a whole of government approach to National security. This type of gap-filling capacity creates the illusion of Defense Department ownership of a function better suited to some other branch of government. Additionally, ad hoc entities such as Joint Interagency Coordinating Groups and the Task Force for Business and Stability Operations are also of limited effectiveness as the Department of Defense cannot compel any other branch of the Executive to act. The result is a bureaucratic organism that improves interagency communications but has limited effectiveness actually bringing to bear all the resources of government. Lastly, the existence of these capabilities under military auspices increases the visibility of American military activity at a time in history when more benevolent tools would alleviate international suspicion.

---

[131] Morris Janowitz, *The Professional Soldier* (New York: The Free Press of Glencoe, 1961), 417.

The United States should also expand the authorities of the National Security Counsel (NSC) to empower it with directive oversight of the American interagency process. Current efforts to ensure a comprehensive approach via the State Department's Coordinator for Reconstruction and Stabilization (CRS) are laudable, but doomed to failure.[132] First, assigning primacy of a supposed whole-of-government planning effort to a State Department organization ensures constant inter-departmental infighting, with only the Secretary of State to adjudicate. Also, the CRS is several echelons below key decision-makers, so arriving at decisions for a comprehensive government response is overwhelmingly burdensome. Professionalizing key positions within the NSC and codifying the primacy of the National Security Advisor in directing interagency efforts will ensure continuity in American foreign policy and would "create the capability to integrate and apply all of the elements of national power" called for by Secretary Gates.[133] With such a framework, the United States would then be well-postured to develop and synchronize whole-of-government approaches to problems or crises.[134]

Leadership in Multilateralism

"No nation's security and wellbeing can be lastingly achieved in isolation, but only in effective cooperation with fellow nations."

Dwight D. Eisenhower[135]

---

[132] President, National Security Presidential Directive 44, "Management of Interagency Efforts Concerning Reconstruction and Stabilization," 7 December 2005.

[133] Gates, Landon Lecture, 26 November 2007.

[134] Germany established its "Crisis Response Centre of the Federal Foreign Office" to facilitate a comprehensive government response to crises. The center is manned by representatives from throughout the federal government who are provided specialized training to "expand interministerial cooperation." For more on Germany's strategy for building a comprehensive crisis capability see the Ministry of Defense's *White Paper 2006* (Cologne: J.P. Bachem GmbH & Co. KG), October 2006, or at http://www.bmvg.de/portal/a/bmvg/kcxml/04_Sj9SPykssy0xPLMnMz0vM0Y_QjzKLd4k38XYGSYGZbu b6kTCxoJRUfW99X4_83FT9AP2C3IhyR0dFRQAflmJV/delta/base64xml/L0IKWWttUSEhL3dITUFDc0 FJVUFOby80SUVhREFBIS9lbg!!

[135] Benita Ferrero-Waldner, (lecture at the Center for Strategic and International Studies, Washington, D.C., 13 January 2005), http://www.eurunion.org/news/press/2005/2005006.htm (accessed 14 December 2007).

Rogue-America pundits often cite American actions to limit, counter, or otherwise disregard the United Nations as evidence of its arrogant disregard for world order and rule of law. This however, presumes the integrity of the United Nations as beyond reproach. The United Nations is, however, "imperfect and rather impervious to reform" and so frequently subject to manipulation by those countries with an axe to grind rather than as a forum to implement positive international action.[136] Indeed, Erik Voeten's research suggests countries in the United Nations increasingly "punish uncooperative [American] behavior" by introducing "resolutions to renounce unilateralist U.S. policies and drop[ping] resolutions supportive of U.S. purposes."[137] Still, as the multilateral body recognized as the world's authority for global security, the United Nations should continue to be America's primary vehicle for international crisis resolution.

As noted earlier, the current world order reflects that of its American architects. As such, the elements of multilateralism inherent in the American political system are equally important in the global one. The active, deep and sustained dialog between liberals and conservatives, isolationists and federalists is at the heart of America's success. So too, is this multilateral approach to American foreign policy necessary to sustain its long history of "pragmatism and flexibility." The interwar years and the decade after the Cold War stand as reminders of the incoherent National strategy that results when the United States government deviates from its history of vigorous multilateral discourse.[138] To cede leadership in the global multilateral discourse to another sovereign will surely accelerate the exploitation of rogue-America rhetoric from competitors seeking an alternative world order.

The United States should redouble efforts to highlight its leadership in multilateral solutions to international challenges. In one of the few areas idealists and realists agree, America

---

[136] Soros, *Bubble of American Supremacy,* 118.

[137] Voeten. "Resisting the Lonely Superpower," 747.

[138] Mead, *Special Providence,* 312, 320.

cannot go it alone.[139] More importantly, America must avoid the perception of going it alone.

This is not to suggest the United States should abandon the historical exceptionalism that is at the

core of its global leadership. Nor should the United States embrace the idealistic multilateralism

emphasizing the "virtues of cooperation among states" that (arguably) led to the demise of the

Soviet Union from within.[140] On the contrary, the United States should return to the essence of

that leadership which forged international consensus when crises emerge. This is not the

Clausewitzian leadership of "high ambition" pursued with "audacity and strength of will."[141]

Rather, it the leadership of Eisenhower in "getting someone else to do something you want done

because he wants to do it."[142] This is leadership grounded in the liberal realism that has served

the United States so well for its entire history.

---

[139] Joseph S. Nye, *Understanding International Conflicts* (New York: Longman, 2003), 252; Huntington, "The Lonely Superpower," 37

[140] Mearsheimer, *Tragedy of Great Power Politics*, 202.

[141] Carl Von Clausewitz, *Principles of War* (New York: Courier Dover Publications, 2003), 65.

[142] John Antonakis et al., *The Nature of Leadership* (London: Sage Publications, 2004), 126.

BIBLIOGRAPHY

Aita, Judy. "Holbrooke: Iraq Will Be a Major UN Issue for Bush Administration," Excerpted from press conference by Richard Holbrooke, outgoing United States Ambassador to the United Nations, 11 January 2001, http://www.usembassy.it/file2001_01/alia/a1011102.htm (accessed 17April 2008).

Antonakis, John. *The Nature of Leadership.* London: Sage Publications, 2004.

Associated Press, "U.S. Diplomats in Uproar," *Kansas City Star,* 1 November 2007.

Berenger, Ralph D., ed., *Global Media Go To War: Role of News and Entertainment Media During the 2003 Iraq War.* Spokane: Marquette Books, 2004.

Birtle, Andrew J. *U.S. Army Counterinsurgency and Contingency Operations Doctrine 1860-1941,* Center of Military History, United States Army, Washington, D.C., 1998

Blum, William. *Killing Hope: U.S. Military and CIA Intervention Since World War II*, 2nd ed. Monroe: Common Courage Press, 2003

---. *Rogue State: A Guide to the World's Only Superpower.* Monroe: Common Courage Press, 2000.

Boggs, Carl. *Masters of War.* New York: Routledge, 2003

Boniface, Pascal. "Reflections on America as a World Power: a European View," *Journal of Palestine Studies* 29, no. 3 (Spring 2000).

Brinkley, Paul. "A Cause for Hope: Economic Revitalization in Iraq," *Military Review* 87, no. 4 (July-August 2007)

Bunting, Madeleine. "Beginning of the End: The U.S. is Ignoring an Important Lesson from History," *Guardian,* 3 February 2003, http://www.guardian.co.uk/world/2003/feb/03/usa.comment, (accessed 22 February 2008).

Burke, Edmund. "Remarks on the Policy of the Allies With Respect to France," *The Works of the Right Honourable Edmund Burke Vol. III*, George Bell and Sons, 1887, page 448. http://books.google.com/books?id=LJALAAAAIAAJ&pg=PA410&lpg=PA410&dq=burke+%22remarks+on+the+policy+of+the+allies%22&source=web&ots=1bHgm3l0vX&sig=AAVs4p-a5jf3WEfPmq0SNYyAhy0&hl=en#PPA448,M1 (accessed 8 January 2008)

Bush, George W. Speech from the USS Abraham Lincoln, 1 May 2003, http://www.whitehouse.gov/news/releases/2003/05/20030501-15.html, (accessed 21 January 2008).

The Central Intelligence Agency, Factbook, Pakistan page, 20 March 2008 https://www.cia.gov/library/publications/the-world-factbook/geos/pk.html#People (accessed 25 March 2008).

The Central Intelligence Agency, Factbook, China page, 15 April 2008, https://www.cia.gov/library/publications/the-world-factbook/geos/ch.html (accessed 23 April 2008).

Chomsky, Noam. *9-11.* New York: Seven Stories Press, 2001.

---. *Rogue States.* Cambridge: South End Press, 2000.

---. "Rogue States Draw the Usual Line," *The Noam Chomsky Website,* May 2001, http://www.chomsky.info/interviews/200105--.htm (accessed 3 August 2007).

Clausewitz, Carl Von. *Principles of War.* New York: Courier Dover Publications, 2003.

Conquest, Robert. "Revisioning Stalin's Russia," *Russian Review* 46, no. 4 (October 1987).

Dunne, Michael. "Hemisphere and the Globe: the Terms of American Foreign Relations," *International Affairs* 70, no. 4 (October 1994).

Eder, Mari K. Brigadier General, U.S. Army. "Toward Strategic Communication," *Military Review* 87, no. 4 (July-August 2007).

Ferrero-Waldner, Benita. Lecture at the Center for Strategic and International Studies, Washington, D.C., 13 January 2005, http://www.eurunion.org/news/press/2005/2005006.htm (accessed 14 December 2007).

---. "Opportunities and Challenges in the EU-US Relationship." Lecture, French-American Foundation, New York, 28 September 2007, http://www.eurunion.org/news/press/2005/2005006.htm (accessed 14 December 2007).

Friedman, Thomas L. *The Lexus and the Olive Tree.* New York: Farrar, Straus, Giroux, New York, 1999.

---. *The World Is Flat.* New York: Farrar, Straus and Giroux, 2005.

Fukuyama, Francis. *The End of History and the Last Man Standing.* New York: Perennial, 2002.

Gates, Robert M. Landon Lecture, Kansas State University, 26 November 2007, http://www.america.gov/st/texttrans-english/2007/November/20071206191908bpuh0.9181177.html, (accessed 21 February 2008).

Halloran, Richard. "Strategic Communication," *Parameters* 37, no 3, Autumn 2007.

Hamilton, Alexander and Madison, James. *The Federalist Papers.* New York: Bantam Books, 1982.

Henderson, Simon. "Saudi Arabia: the Nightmare of Iraq," *With Neighbors Like These: Iraq and the Arab States on Its Borders,* Policy Focus #70, The Washington Institute for Near East Policy, June 2007.

Herspring, Dale R. *The Pentagon and the Presidency: Civil-Military Relations From FDR to George W. Bush.* Lawrence: University Press of Kansas, 2005.

Holbrooke, Richard. *To End a War.* New York: The Modern Library, 1999.

Howeidy, Amira. "After Baghdad, Is Cairo Next?" *Al Jazeera,* (18 January 2006), http://english.aljazeera.net/English/Archive/Archive?ArchiveID=17755 (accessed 19 September 2007)

Huntington, Samuel P. "The Lonely Superpower," *Foreign Policy* 78, no. 2 (March/Apil 1999).

Janowitz, Morris, *The Professional Soldier: A Social and Political Portrait,* The Free Press, 1961.

Johnson, Chalmers A. *The Sorrows of Empire.* New York: Metropolitan Books, 2004

Johnson, Chalmers A. *Blowback.* Holt Paperbacks, 2001

Killigrew, John W. "The Army and the Bonus Incident," *Military Affairs* 26, no. 2 (Summer 1962)

Kinzer, Stephen. *Overthrow: America's Century of Regime Change from Hawaii to Iraq.* New York: Henry Holt and Company, 2006

Klare, Michael. *Rogue States and Nuclear Outlaws: America's Search for a New Foreign Policy.* New York: Hill and Wang, 1995.

Korean Central News Agency, "US Termed Facist and Rogue State," (March 8, 2003), http://www.globalsecurity.org/wmd/library/news/dprk/2003/dprk-030310-kcna06.htm (accessed November 16, 2007).

Lake, Anthony. "The Reach of Democracy: Tying Power to Diplomacy," *New York Times* (23 September 1994), http://query.nytimes.com/gst/fullpage.html?res=9D07E3D7143AF930A1575AC0A96295 8260&sec=&spon=&pagewanted=2, (accessed 21 January 2008).

The Library of Congress, "America's Story: Boston Massacre," *America's Library,* http://www.americaslibrary.gov/cgi-bin/page.cgi/jb/revolut/boston_1.

Litwak, Robert S. *Rogue States and U.S. Foreign Policy.* Washington, D.C.: Woodrow Wilson Center Press, 2000.

Lowe, Robert and Spencer, Claire. "Iran, Its Neighbours and the Regional Crises," Chatham House (The Royal Institute of International Affairs), 2006.

Mandelbaum, Michael. "Democracy Without America: the Spontaneous Spread of Freedom," *Foreign Affairs* 86, no. 5 (September/October 2007).

Mann, Michael. *Incoherent Empire.* New York: Verso, 2003.

Maksoud, Clovis, "The Future of Arab-U.S. Relations: Problems and Prospects," speech to the Los Angeles World Affairs Council, 20 September 2007, http://www.lawac.org/speech/indexes/2007-08_index.htm (accessed 19 December 2007).

Matar, Gamil. "A Marriage Made in Hell," *Al Ahram Weekly,* 5 April 2006, http://weekly.ahram.org.eg/2006/788/op2.htm (accessed 19 January 2008).

Mazarr, Michael J. "The Long Road to Pyongyang: A Case Study in Policymaking Without Direction," *Foreign Affairs* 86, no. 5 (September/October 2007).

McDougall, Walter A. *Promised Land, Crusader State.* Boston: Houghton Mifflin Company, 1997.

Mead, Walter Russell. *Special Providence: American Foreign Policy and How it Changed the World.* New York: Taylor & Francis Books, 2002.

Mearsheimer, John J. *The Tragedy of Great Power Politics.* New York: W.W. Norton & Company, 2001

Merriam-Webster's Online dictionary http://www.m-w.com/dictionary/rogue (accessed 30 January 2008).

Miller, Linda B. "The Clinton Years: Reinventing US Foreign Policy," *International Affairs* 70, no. 4 (October 1994).

Millett, Allan R. and Maslowski, Peter. *For the Common Defense: A Military History of the United States of America.* New York: The Free Press, 1984.

Minnerop, Petra. "Rogue States-State Sponsors of Terrorism?" German Law Journal 3, no. 9 (1 September 2002) http://www.germanlawjournal.com/article.php?id=188 (accessed 16 November 2007)

Murphy, Sean D. *Humanitarian Intervention: the United Nations in an Evolving World Order.* Philadelphia: University of Pennsylvania Press, 1996.

Nova Television. "Former Dutch PM Wants Iraq Pull-Out," *Al Jazeera,* (27 April 2004), http://english.aljazeera.net/English/Archive/Archive?ArchiveID=3340 (accessed 19 September 2007)

Nowels, Larry. "Foreign Aid: Understanding Data Used to Compare Donors," CRS Report for Congress, 23 May 2005.

Nye, Joseph S. *The Paradox of American Power.* New York: Oxford University Press, 2002.

---. *Understanding International Conflicts.* New York: Longman, 2003.

Office of National AIDS Policy. "President's HIV/AIDS Initiatives," The White House, http://www.whitehouse.gov/infocus/hivaids (accessed 28 April 2008).

Pak, Jin H. "China's Pragmatic Rise: and U.S. Interests in East Asia," *Military Review* 87, no. 6 (November-December 2007)

Patten, Chris. Cyril Foster Lecture, Balliol College, Oxford, 30 January 2003, http://ec.europa.eu/external_relations/news/patten/oxford300103.htm (accessed 14 December 2007)

---. "Europe and America: Has the Transatlantic Relationship Run Out of Road?" Lecture, Lady Margaret Hall, Oxford, 13 February 2004, http://ec.europa.eu/external_relations/news/patten/sp04_77.htm (accessed 24 January 2008)

Pirzada, Moeed. "Post Election Fault Lines," *Khaleej Times,* 28 Febrary 2008, http://www.khaleejtimes.com/DisplayArticleNew.asp?section=opinion&xfile=data/opinion/2008/february/opinion_february108.xml (accessed 25 March 2008).

Price, Tom. *Cyber Activism: Advocacy Groups and the Internet.* Washington D.C.: Foundation for Public Affairs, 2000.

Public Broadcasting Service, *Empires,* http://www.pbs.org/empires/ (accessed 30 January 2008).

Rankin, Jennifer. "Is America a Rogue State?" *The Foreign Policy Centre* (2003), http://fpc.org.uk/fsblob/247.pdf (accessed 25 January 2008).

Rosefielde, Steven. "Incriminating Evidence: Excess Deaths and Forced Labour under Stalin: A Final Reply to Critics," *Soviet Studies* 39, no. 2 (April 1987).

Roy, Denny. "China's Pitch for a Multipolar World," *Asia-Pacific Center for Security Studies* 2, no. 1 (May 2003): 2.

Rubin, Barry. "U.S. Foreign Policy and Rogue States," *Middle East Review of International Affairs* 3, no. 3 (September 1999), http://meria.idc.ac.il/journal/1999/issue3/jv3n3a7.html (accessed 30 January 2008).

The Russian Federation. "National Security Blueprint," January 2000, as translated by the U.S. Foreign Broadcast Information Service and excerpted in *Arms Control Today,* January/February 2000, http://www.armscontrol.org/act/2000_01-02/docjf00.asp (accessed 23 January 2008).

Soros, George. *The Bubble of American Supremacy.* Public Affairs, 2004

Thomas, Landon, Jr. "Dread of American Downturn Goes Global," *Kansas City Star,* 22 January 2008

United States Holocaust Memorial Museum, "The Holocaust," *Holocaust Encyclopedia,* http://www.ushmm.org/wlc/article.php?lang=en&ModuleId=10005143 (accessed 23 April 2008).

U.S. Department of Defense. *Directive Number 3000.05,*"Military Support for Stability, Security, Transition, and Reconstruction (SSTR) Operations." Washington, DC, 28 November 2005

U.S. Department of State, "China Country Report on Human Rights Practices for 2007," http://www.state.gov/g/drl/rls/hrrpt/2007/100518.htm (accessed 23 April 2008).

U.S. President. National Security Presidential Directive 44, "Management of Interagency Efforts Concerning Reconstruction and Stabilization" (7 December 2005).

---. *The National Security Strategy of the United States of America* (March 2006).

---. *The National Security Strategy of the United States of America* (September 2002).

Voeten, Erik. "Resisting the Lonely Superpower: Responses of States in the United Nations to U.S. Dominance," *The Journal of Politics* 66, no. 3 (August 2004).

Washington Post. "Hussein Mistook American Intentions," *Kansas City Star,* 27 January 2008.